# Homonyms

*When You Need to Write the Right Words*


By Kathy Zengolewicz

Photos on cover, page 7 and 9 are credited to istockphoto.com.

www.kathyzengolewicz.com.

Manufactured in the United States of America.

ISBN 978-0-615-37795-7

# ƒoreword

As an editor, writer, linguist, and teacher, I've always been fascinated by language and how its speakers use the words in the lexicon. Questions I've often pondered about American English in particular include: what determines the number of syllables a word has; is there some formula hidden in the grammar of the language that, unbeknownst to its speakers, dictates syllabification? Do certain types of words have an even number of syllables while other, different types have an odd number of syllables? Why do we have so many words to mean almost the same thing? Why do some areas of the U.S.A. say "pop" for a carbonated beverage while others say "soda" or even "soda pop"?

I have found the answers to many of my questions; some are still left unanswered. Homonyms are one of those fascinating subjects, which, when researched, can immerse me in the mysteries of American English for hours.

Homonyms, such as, their or there, buy, by, or bye, and hundreds more, are often misused. Have you ever misused one? If you have, you are not alone! I have 30 years professional experience using the American English language, and I still get some homonyms confused. And, don't count on the spell check feature of your software, because these words are spelled correctly! As I tell my ESL (English as a Second Language) students, when in doubt, look it up.

A quick perusal of the printed and online lexicons of the language yields these broad definitions of homonyms: Homonyms and homophones are one of two or more words that have the same sound and often the same spelling but differ in meaning (for example, to, too, two).

Confusion often reigns (note: not *rains*), however, about the difference between *homonyms* and *homophones*. Whenever I need the definitive answer to something, I go to the experts: The Linguist List (http://linguistlist.org).

In answer to the question: What is a homonym? The Linguist List refers us to SIL International, which provides a Glossary of Linguistic Terms (at http://www.sil.org/linguistics/GlossaryOflinguisticTerms/WhatIsAHomonym.htm). This glossary defines a homonym as "a word that has the same pronunciation as another. Homonyms differ from each other in:

- meaning
- origin, and
- usually spelling."

However, the SIL glossary states that homonyms are also known, as, you guessed it, *homophones*! And, are "loosely" called *homographs*, which are words with the same spelling but different in meaning.

Let's look at some examples they give:
- Words with the same pronunciation but different in meaning:
  - o *bore* and *boar* (wait, what about *boor*?)
  - o *two* and *too*
- Homographs:
  - o *bow*: to bend
  - o *bow*: a decorative knot

So, what about homophones? According to the glossary, a homophone is "a group of two or more letters representing the same speech sound, or a homonym."

Let's look at the examples they give:
- Letters with the same speech sound:
  - o *c* in *city*
  - o *s* in *song*
- Homonyms:
  - o *two* and *too*

Hence, some homophones are also homonyms. Whereas homonyms focus on the meaning, origin, and, usually, spelling differences for the same sound, homophones focus on the *letter* differences with the same speech sound, and, homographs focus on the different meanings for the same *spelling*! It's easy to see why native speakers of American English get confused about the trio, let alone those brave people who are trying to learn English as another language!

I find that when I am trying to make sense of the American English language, a table helps:

| Word | Same Whole Word Sound | Same Spelling | Same Letter Sound | Same Meaning |
|------|----------------------|---------------|-------------------|--------------|
| Homonym | Yes | No, not usually | Yes | No |
| Homograph | Yes | Yes | Yes | No |
| Homophone | No | No | Yes | No |

I hope that helps. Either way, enjoy Kathy's book. It is a handy and easy-to-use reference for anyone trying to get their ~~pause~~ paws on and ~~clause~~ claws into these pesky ~~purls~~ pearls and ~~pares pears~~ pairs!

*Sue Kern*, M.A., English Linguistics
Founder and Director
The Writer's Cottage

# *I*ntroduction

**H**omonyms have fascinated me since I was a second grade student just learning to explore language and grammar. At that time, I couldn't grasp the fact that two words were spelled and pronounced the same, but had different meanings. It was a few years later when I determined that these were complex words that could be understood through study.

A few years later I began to realize how important homonyms were, especially to a writer. My fascination grew and I began researching more and more. I not only studied the words, they became a part of my being. The more I lost myself in my writing, the more important words became in my everyday life.

After a while, I started to notice every wrong word that someone spoke or read. It became very difficult to hear or see someone use a homonym in the wrong way. It has taken me quite some time to make myself vigilant enough to keep my mouth closed and not be a boor when I want to correct someone.

Whether (~~weather~~) you are a writer, high school or college student, and/or a professional who must write at work, this hands-on, ready reference is a must-have tool to support your proper use of the American English language.

So, make this book a part of your home and office reference library, and you'll be on your way to conquering the challenge of American English homonyms!

*Kathy Zengolewicz*

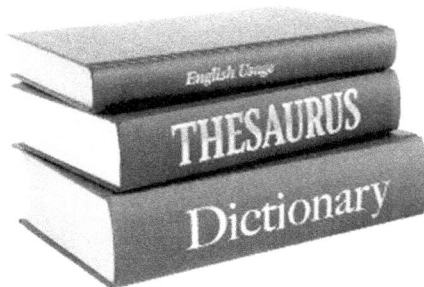

# *A*

**ACCEPT**: to take or receive with approval or favor. *Please **accept** my apology.*
**EXCEPT**: with the exclusion of; excluding. *I'll buy all of those gloves except the red ones.*

∽

**AIR**: a mixture of nitrogen, oxygen, and minute amounts of other gases that surround the earth and form its atmosphere. *The **air** seems to be filled with electricity.*
**HEIR**: a person who inherits or has a right of inheritance in the property of another following the latter's death. *He is the **heir** to the family's fortune.*

∽

**AISLE**: a walkway between or along sections of seats in a theater, classroom, or the like. *Her father walked her down the **aisle** when she married.*
**I'LL**: contraction of "I will". *I'll cook the dinner for the celebration.*
**ISLE**: a small island. *She vacationed on an **isle** in the Caribbean.*

∽

**ALL**: the whole of, every. *Pack **all** of those supplies together.*
**AWL**: a pointed instrument for piercing small holes in leather, wood, etc. *He used the **awl** to punch another hole in his belt.*

∽

**ALLOWED**: to give permission to or for; permit. *Were you **allowed** to go to the fair?*
**ALOUD**: vocally, as distinguished from mentally. *He gave his presentation **aloud**.*

∽

**ALLUDE**: to refer casually or indirectly, a casual or indirect reference. *Her comments **alluded** to an earlier discussion..*
**ELUDE**: to avoid or escape by speed, cleverness or trickery. *He tried to **elude** the speeding car.*

∽

**ANT**: any of numerous black, red, brown, or yellow social insects. *I have never been on a picnic where I didn't see at least one **ant**.*
**AUNT**: the sister of one's father or mother. *Her **aunt** came to visit her last week.*

**ATE**: having eaten or digested. *The weary travelers **ate** in silence.*
**EIGHT**: a cardinal number, seven plus one. *Joan will be **eight** years old tomorrow.*

**AYE**: an affirmative vote or voter, esp. in British Parliament. *At last count, the vote was one **aye** and three nays.*

**EYE**: the organ of sight. *The wind blew dirt into his **eye**.*

**I**: the ninth letter of the English alphabet, a vowel. *I will call your office on Tuesday.*

# *B*

**BALL**: a spherical or approximately spherical body or shape; sphere. *Throw the* **ball** *to Billy.*
**BAWL**: to utter or proclaim by outcry; shout out. *At the mention of the lost keys, she started to* **bawl***.*

∽

**BAND**: a musical group. *My brother just joined a rock* **band***.*
**BANNED**: to prohibit, forbid, or bar. *The chemical pesticide DDT is a* **banned** *insecticide.*

∽

**BEACH**: an expanse of sand or pebbles along a shore. *They played on the* **beach** *all day.*
**BEECH**: any tree of temperate regions, having a smooth gray bark and bearing small, edible, triangular nuts. *We recently planted* **beech** *trees in front of our house.*

∽

**BARE**: without covering or clothing. The ordinarily ornate basket was bare today.
**BEAR**: (v) to hold up or support. (v) *He could not* **bear** *the stress of working there.* (n) large mammal found in North America, South America, Europe and Asia. (n) *We came face to face with a huge black* **bear***.*

∽

**BASE**: the bottom support of something. *The* **base** *of the statue was made of plastic.*
**BASS**: of the lowest pitch or range. *He played the* **bass** *guitar in the band.*

∽

**BE**: to exist or live. *We should* **be** *grateful for the help of the others.*
**BEE**: any hymenopterous insect of the superfamily, Apoidea, or a community social gathering in order to perform some task. *Her arm became red after being stung by the* **bee***.*

∽

**BELL**: a hollow instrument of cast metal. *You need to ring the* **bell** *for service.*
**BELLE**: a woman or girl admired for her beauty and charm. *She was a regular southern* **belle***.*

∽

**BERRY**: a pulpy and usually edible fruit of small. *The* **berry** *plant was in full bloom.*
**BURY**: to put in the ground and cover with earth. *The dog tried to* **bury** *his bone in the flowerbed.*

**BERTH**: a shelf-like sleeping space, as on a ship, airplane, or railroad car. *Joe wanted to sleep in his own **berth** when we traveled to Maryland by train.*
**BIRTH**: an act or instance of being born. *We witnessed the **birth** of a kangaroo at the zoo while on vacation.*

✇

**BILLED**: having a bill or beak. A statement of money owed for goods or service. *His credit card was **billed** for the hotel room.*
**BUILD**: to construct by assembling parts or materials. *They had all of the materials to **build** the house.*

✇

**BLEW**: past tense of blow; (of the wind or air) to be in motion. *They **blew** up the party balloons too early.*
**BLUE**: the primary color between green and violet in the visible spectrum. *They repainted the baby's nursery a light **blue** color.*

✇

**BOAR**: an uncastrated male swine. *Wild **boar** roam freely in some parts of Europe.*
**BOOR**: a churlish, rude, or unmannerly person. *The man she is dating is a real **boor**.*
**BORE**: to pierce (a solid substance) with some rotary cutting instrument, or a dull, tiresome, or uncongenial person. *He tried to **bore** into the wall with a screwdriver.*

✇

**BOARD**: a flat slab of wood or other material. *We placed the **board** over the hole in the deck.*
**BORED**: to make weary by being dull, repetitive, or tedious. *The children were **bored** with the activities.*

✇

**BORN**: brought forth by birth. *She was **born** in Michigan.*
**BORNE**: past particle of bear (to hold up or support). *The article was about mosquito-borne diseases.*

**BOUGH**: a branch of a tree, esp. one of the larger or main branches. *The **bough** of the tree nearly broke due to the high winds.*
**BOW**: to bend the knee or body or incline the head, as in reverence, submission, salutation, recognition, or acknowledgment. ***Bow** your head when praying.*

✇

**BOY**: a male child. *The **boy** fell in the mud puddle.*
**BUOY**: nautical; a distinctively-shaped and marked float. *Let's swim out to the **buoy** and back.*

**BRAKE**: a device for slowing or stopping a vehicle. *Slow down slightly before stepping on the **brake**.*
**BREAK**: to smash, split, or divide into parts violently. *Try not to **break** the seal on the can.*

❧

**BREAD**: food or sustenance; livelihood. *Remember to buy **bread** when you go to the grocery store.*
**BRED**: past tense of breed (to produce or reproduce). *Those horses were **bred** to race.*

❧

**BRIDAL**: of, for, or pertaining to a bride or a wedding. *There were eight people in the **bridal** party.*
**BRIDLE**: part of the tack or harness of a horse. *Hold the **bridle** tightly when riding the horse.*

❧

**BROACH**: (n) a spit for roasting meat. (n) *Place the chicken on the **broach** so that we can begin roasting.* (v) to mention or suggest. (v) *Do not **broach** the subject of politics with him.*
**BROOCH**: a clasp or ornament having a pin at the back for passing through the clothing. *The **brooch** has been handed down through the family for generations.*

❧

**BUT**: unless; if not; except that. *You may play with all of the games **but** that one.*
**BUTT**: the end or extremity of anything. *Through no fault of his own, he became the **butt** of many jokes.*

❧

**BUY**: to acquire the possession of, or the right to, by paying or promising to pay. *I need to go out and **buy** milk from the grocery store.*
**BY**: near to or next to. *He walks **by** the tailor shop on his way to work.*
**BYE**: good-bye. *The baby has just learned how to wave **bye**.*

# *C*

**CAPITAL**: the city or town that is the official seat of government in a country, state, etc. or any source of profit. *Harrisburg is the capital of Pennsylvania.*
**CAPITOL**: the building in Washington, D.C., used by the Congress of the U.S. for its sessions. *The American flag always flies outside of our Capitol in Washington, D.C.*

✑

**CAST**: to throw or hurl. *He cast out the first baseball of the season.*
**CASTE**: any rigid system of social distinctions. *The caste system in India places social restrictions on its citizens.*

✑

**CEILING**: the overhead interior surface of a room. *The bedroom ceiling needs to be repaired.*
**SEALING**: to fasten or close tightly by or as if by a seal. *Someone should be sealing these envelopes to prepare them for posting.*

✑

**CELL**: (n) a small room. (n)*The dangerous prisoner was confined to the cell.*
(n) A small group acting as a unit. (n) *He was a member of a terrorist cell.*
(n) The smallest living organism. (n) *An atom is made up of more than one cell.*
**SELL**: exchange an object for money. *They will sell that property soon.*

✑

**CELLAR**: a room, or set of rooms, for the storage of food, fuel, etc. *The old house had a coal bin in the front of the cellar.*
**SELLER**: a person who sells; salesperson, or vendor. *The settlement fee is being paid by the property seller.*

✑

**CENT**: monetary; a penny. *Don't spend another cent of your money on those soft drinks.*
**SCENT**: a distinctive odor, most times agreeable. *The room was filled with the scent of lemon from the newly placed freshener.*
**SENT**: past tense of send. *She sent her payment through the mail.*

✑

**CEREAL**: a plant (as a grass) yielding farinaceous grain suitable for food. *Most mornings, I eat cold cereal for breakfast.*
**SERIAL**: anything published, broadcast, etc., in short installments at regular intervals. *She was presently watching a serial program about wildlife.*

**CHANCE**: a possibility; a gamble. *Is there a **chance** she will appear? Let's take a **chance** to win that basket.*
**CHANTS**: short simple melodies. *You could hear the **chants** throughout the room.*

∽

**CHEAP**: costing very little. *The clothes she wore were **cheap** and of poor quality.*
**CHEEP**: to chirp; peep. *The baby bird would **cheep** loudly when he was hungry.*

∽

**CHEWS**: to crush or grind with the teeth. *She **chews** her food thoroughly before swallowing.*
**CHOOSE**: to select from a number of possibilities. *Who would you **choose** to go to the tournament?*

∽

**CHORD**: (n) a feeling or emotion. *His story struck a **chord** of pity in the listeners.* (n) a combination of usually three or more musical tones sounded simultaneously. (n) *He struck the **cord** with little or no problem.* (v) to play a chord, harmonize or voice. (v) *How would you **chord** that in B flat?*
**CORD**: any influence that binds or restrains. *His hands were tied behind his back with a **cord**.*

∽

**CITE**: to quote an authority; refer to as an example. *If you are writing a quote, make sure to **cite** the author who first said it.*
**SIGHT**: the power or faculty of seeing. *The gift of **sight** is one of the five senses.*
**SITE**: the position or location of a town or building as to its environment. *The new building will sit on the **site** at the corner.*

∽

**CLAUSE**: a distinct article or provision in a contract. *Make sure to read the **clause** in the fine print before signing the contract.*
**CLAWS**: sharp, usually curved, nails on the feet of animals. *The dog needs his **claws** clipped by the groomer.*

∽

**CLOSE**: to block or hinder access. *Please **close** the door when you leave.*
**CLOTHES**: garments for the body. *Her **clothes** were made of cotton.*

∽

**CLICK**: a slight, sharp sound. *The lock will **click** into place if you close the lid correctly.*
**CLIQUE**: a small, exclusive group of people. *Belonging to a **clique** can be considered snobbish.*

18

**COARSE**: composed of relatively large parts or particles. *That salt has a very* **coarse** *grain.*
**COURSE**: the path, route, or channel along which anything moves. *You can choose the* **course** *that fits your needs.*

~

**COMPLEMENT**: something that completes or makes perfect. *That shirt will* **complement** *your new shoes.*
**COMPLIMENT**: an expression of praise, commendation, or admiration. *She accepted the* **compliment** *with grace.*

~

**CORE**: the central, innermost, or most essential part of anything. *Don't eat the* **core** *of the apple; it doesn't taste good.*
**CORPS**: a military organization consisting of officers and enlisted personnel. *His brother is a member of the Army Air* **Corps**.

~

**COUNCIL**: an assembly of persons summoned or convened for consultation. *The condo association has a safety* **council** *in place.*
**COUNSEL**: advice, opinion or instruction given in directing the judgment or conduct of another. *When you feel alone or afraid, you should seek* **counsel** *from a professional.*

~

**CREAK**: to make a grating or a squeaking sound. *That door will* **creak** *loudly when it opens.*
**CREEK**: a stream or channel of water. *The* **creek** *ran directly behind the cabin.*

~

**CUE**: anything said or done, on or off stage, that is followed by a specific line or action. *Make sure to say your lines on* **cue** *from the director.*
**QUEUE**: a file or line, esp. of people waiting their turn. Typically, used in British English. *The document was in the* **queue** *to print from that system.*

~

**CURRANT**: a small seedless raisin used in cookery and confectionery. *She made a dessert that was filled with a sweet* **currant**.
**CURRENT**: passing in time; belonging to the time actually passing. *Stay* **current** *with the newsletter to please your audience.*

~

**CYMBAL**: a concave plate of brass or bronze that produces a ringing sound when struck. *Strike the* **cymbal** *when you see his hand drop.*
**SYMBOL**: a material object representing something else; emblem; sign. *A large red star is the* **symbol** *for Macy's Department Store.*

# D

**DAYS**: the time between sunrise and sunset. *The **days** grow longer in the summertime.*
**DAZE**: to stun or stupefy with a blow, shock, etc. *She was in a **daze** after being hit in the head with the baseball.*

❧

**DEAR**: beloved or loved. *That ring is very **dear** to my heart.*
**DEER**: hoofed animal in the Cervidae family. *We saw a family of **deer** in the woods, outside of the cottage.*

❧

**DESERT**: an arid region with little or no rainfall. *The Gobi **desert** is in Asia.*
**DESSERT**: cake, pie, fruit, pudding, ice cream, etc. served as a final course of a meal. *I never eat a big **dessert** after a large meal.*

❧

**DEW**: moisture condensed from the atmosphere. *The grass was **dew** covered this morning.*
**DO**: to perform, to execute. *Tell me how you **do** that with your hands.*
**DUE**: owed at present; owing or owed. *The bill is **due** for payment on the first of each month.*

❧

**DIE**: to cease to live. *If you don't water that plant, it will **die**.*
**DYE**: a coloring material or matter. *I can **dye** that blouse a lighter color to match your skirt.*

❧

**DOE**: a female deer. *The **doe** gave birth deep in the forest.*
**DOUGH**: flour or meal combined with water, milk, etc., in a mass for baking into bread or cake. *We need to make the **dough** for the pizza and then put it in the oven.*

❧

**DRAFT**: a drawing, sketch or design; a current of air in any enclosed space in a room. *We will need a **draft** of the proposal.*
**DRAUGHT**: container for drinking; flow of something, usually water. *His preference for beer is a **draught** brew.*

# *E*

**EARN**: to gain or get in return for one's labor or service. *How much can you* **earn** *in that job?*

**URN**: a large decorative vase, especially one with an ornamental foot or pedestal. *The* **urn** *was filled with wildflowers.*

∽

**ELICIT**: to draw or bring forth; to evoke. *He could* **elicit** *the truth from the suspect with ease.*

**ILLICIT**: not legally permitted or authorized; unlawful. *She has been accused of* **illicit** *behavior while at work.*

∽

**EWE**: a female sheep when fully mature. *The* **ewe** *was very protective of her young.*

**YEW**: any of several evergreen, coniferous trees and shrubs. *They planted a* **yew** *shrub in the garden.*

**YOU**: the pronoun of the second person singular or plural, used for the person being addressed. *Will* **you** *attend the concert?*

∽

**EYE**: the organ of sight. *Her* **eye** *color is a light brown.*

**I**: the ninth letter of the English alphabet; the nominative singular pronoun. *I think you are right to choose the underdog.*

# F

**FACTS**: something that actually exists; reality; truth. *The facts of the situation are clear.*
**FAX**: transmit printed matter electronically. *Fax the information to our branch office.*

❧

**FAIN**: happily, gladly, willingly. *He was fain to obey the rules.*
**FEIGN**: to represent fictitiously; put on an appearance of. *Don't feign innocence where there is nothing but guilt.*

❧

**FAINT**: lacking brightness, vividness or clearness; to lose consciousness temporarily. *She felt faint from lack of oxygen.*
**FEINT**: a movement made in order to deceive an adversary. *He performed his magic act by feint of hand.*

❧

**FAIR**: free from bias, dishonesty, or injustice. *Always be fair in your judgment of people.*
**FARE**: the price of conveyance or passage in a bus, train, airplane, or other vehicle. *The bus fare has risen steadily over the last few years.*

❧

**FAIRY**: in folklore, one of a class of supernatural beings. *The fairy alighted on her finger.*
**FERRY**: a commercial service with terminals and boats for transporting persons, automobiles, etc., across a river or other comparatively small body of water. *They rode the ferry across the river.*

❧

**FAZE**: to cause to be disturbed or disconcerted. *The outcome didn't seem to faze him.*
**PHASE**: a stage in a process of change or development. *Which phase of the project have you just completed?*

❧

**FEAT**: a noteworthy or extraordinary act or achievement, usually displaying boldness or skill. *That presentation is a feat to be remembered.*
**FEET**: plural of foot; terminal part of the leg, below the ankle joint, on which the body stands. *Stand on your own two feet and you will succeed.*

**FILE**: a folder, cabinet or other container in which papers, etc., are arranged for storage. *Place those papers in the **file** for safekeeping.*
**PHIAL**: a container, usually for liquids. *Fill the **phial** with the water from that container.*

❧

**FIND**: to come upon by chance. *Where did he **find** his keys?*
**FINED**: penalized for wrongdoing. *He was **fined** for littering.*

❧

**FIR**: any coniferous tree in the pine family with flat needles and erect cones. *We decorated the **fir** tree with bright lights.*
**FUR**: the fine, soft, thick, hairy coat of the skin of a mammal. *She received a **fur** coat for her birthday.*

❧

**FLAIR**: a natural talent, aptitude or ability; smartness of style or manner. *He had a **flair** for creating lovely centerpieces.*
**FLARE**: to burn with an unsteady, swaying flame, as a torch or a candle in the wind. *Each time the wind blew, the fire would **flare** with new life.*

❧

**FLEA**: a small, wingless bloodsucking insect. *The dog had a **flea** on his nose.*
**FLEE**: to run away, as from danger or pursuers. *They had to **flee** for their lives when the fire broke out.*

❧

**FLEW**: took to the air, usually employing wings. *The bird **flew** off into the distance.*
**FLU**: a specific variety of influenza, an illness. *He missed three days at school because he had the **flu**.*
**FLUE**: a passage or duct for smoke in a chimney. *The chimney **flue** needs to be repaired.*

❧

**FLOCKS**: a number of animals of one kind, especially sheep, goats or birds that feed and herd together. *There were **flocks** of sea gulls on the southern tip of the shore.*
**PHLOX**: a species of plant that is cultivated for its showy flowers and various colors. *She planted the **phlox** around the perimeter of the garden.*

❧

**FLOUR**: the finely ground meal of grain. *We are using rye **flour** to make this bread.*
**FLOWER**: the blossom of a plant. *What is the name of the **flower** in that bouquet?*

**FOR**: with an object or purpose. *He is running **for** office.*
**FOUR**: a cardinal number. *Three plus one is **four**.*

∽

**FOREWORD**: a short introductory statement in a published work, such as a book, when written by someone other than the author. *I need an expert in English to write a **foreword** for my new book.*
**FORWARD**: directed toward a point in advance; moving ahead; onward. *They moved **forward** quickly in the line.*

∽

**FOUL**: grossly offensive to the senses; loathsome. *The spoiled food gave off a **foul** odor.*
**FOWL**: a domestic or barnyard hen or rooster. *Chickens and roosters are considered domestic **fowl**.*

# *H*

**HAIL**: to cheer, salute, or greet; welcome. *Everyone cheered when the band played "**Hail** to the Chief."*
**HALE**: free from disease; robust. *He has grown into a **hale** and hardy young man.*

∽

**HAIR**: fine filaments growing from the skin of humans and animals. *She went to the stylist to have her **hair** cut.*
**HARE**: rodent like mammal having long ears, a divided upper lip and long hind limbs. *Do you remember the story of the tortoise and the **hare**?*

∽

**HAY**: grass, clover, alfalfa, etc. cut and dried for use as forage. *It's time to feed the cows some **hay**.*
**HEY**: an interjection used as an exclamation to call attention to or express surprise or pleasure. ***Hey**, are you the one who won the prize?*

∽

**HEAL**: to restore to health. *Give the wound some time to **heal**.*
**HEEL**: the back part of the human foot, below the ankle. *She has a blister on her **heel** from her new shoes.*

∽

**HEAR**: to perceive by the ear; be informed of; to listen to. *Did you **hear** the latest news about the economy?*
**HERE**: in this place; in this spot or locality. *You can stay **here** while you are visiting.*

∽

**HEARD**: detected by perceiving sound. *She **heard** a loud, crashing sound.*
**HERD**: a number of animals kept, feeding, or traveling together. *We came across a **herd** of sheep while we were hiking.*

∽

**HI**: used as an exclamation of greeting. *They waived **hi** to the children.*
**HIGH**: having great reach upward, elevated. *The apple tree is now 20 feet **high**.*

∽

**HIGHER**: at a great distance aloft; extreme; costly. *Raise the picture **higher** on the wall to make it easier to see.*
**HIRE**: to engage the service of. *When will they **hire** a new waitress?*

**HIM**: the objective case of he. *Give **him** a plate to hold his cake.*
**HYMN**: a song or ode in praise or honor of God, a deity, or a nation. *The choir sung a beautiful **hymn** for the procession.*

✍

**HOAR**: hoarfrost, rime (an opaque coating of tiny white granular ice particles). *The meat had been frozen so long that it acquired a **hoar** coating.*
**WHORE**: a prostitute; harlot; strumpet. *Although she was considered a prostitute, calling her a **whore** seem rude.*

✍

**HOARD**: to accumulate for preservation, future use. *He would **hoard** his money under a mattress in the guest bedroom.*
**HORDE**: a large group, multitude or number. *There was a **horde** of people gathered in the field for the game.*

✍

**HOARSE**: having a raucous voice. *He cheered until he was **hoarse**.*
**HORSE**: a large solid hoofed domestic animal. *He loved to ride his **horse** in the morning.*

✍

**HOES**: a long handled implement having a flat blade used to break up the surface of the ground, destroy weeds, etc. *The **hoes** were lined up beside the barn door.*
**HOSE**: a flexible tube for conveying a liquid to a desired point. *Use the **hose** to clean the mud off of the car.*

✍

**HOLE**: an opening through something; a gap; aperture. *You could see the large **hole** in his sock when he removed his shoe.*
**WHOLE**: comprising the full quantity, amount, extent, etc. undivided; in one piece. *Instead of a slice, she purchased the **whole** pie.*

✍

**HOLY**: recognized as or declared sacred by religious use or authority. *Christmas is considered a **holy** day in the Christian religion.*
**WHOLLY**: entirely; totally; altogether; quite. *They were not **wholly** responsible for the crash.*

✍

**HOUR**: a period of time equal to one twenty-fourth of a day; 60 minutes. *I exercise for one **hour** every day.*
**OUR**: a form of the possessive case of we; belonging to us. ***Our** friends will be visiting us at the end of this week.*

# *I*

**IDLE**: not working or active; unemployed; doing nothing. *His hands were **idle** for too long.*

**IDOL**: an image or other material object representing a deity; a person or thing regarded with blind admiration, adoration, or devotion. *Dorothy was my **idol** when I was a young girl.*

༄

**ITS**: the possessive form of it; belonging to it. *The dog had **its** foot in the wet cement.*

**IT'S**: a contraction of "it is". ***It's** not as important as it originally seemed.*

# *K*

**KNAP**: a swelling or projection; a bulge, bump. *The ball proved to be the **knap** under the blanket.*
**NAP**: to sleep for a short time. *It is time for the baby to take his afternoon **nap**.*

∽

**KNEW**: past of know; to be cognizant or aware of. *She **knew** of the tension between her friends.*
**NEW**: of recent origin, production, or purchase. *He bought himself a **new** pair of shoes, yesterday.*

∽

**KNIGHT**: a mounted soldier serving under a feudal superior in the Middle Ages. *The story was about a **knight** who saved a princess.*
**NIGHT**: the period of darkness between sunset and sunrise. *She only walked her dog at **night**.*

∽

**KNIT**: to become closely and firmly joined; to make a garment by interlocking loops of yarn. *Her grandmother taught her to **knit** when she reached a certain age.*
**NIT**: the egg of a parasitic insect often attached to a hair or a fiber of clothing. *There was a **nit** on the clean blanket.*

∽

**KNOT**: interlacing, twining, looping of a cord or a rope into a tight knob or lump for fastening. *Please, don't **knot** your shoelaces.*
**NOT**: used to express negation, denial, refusal, or prohibition. *She is **not** an educated person.*
**NAUGHT**: nothing, worthless. *All of his work was for **naught**.*

∽

**KNOW**: to perceive or understand as a fact. *I **know** the combination of the office safe.*
**NO**: a denial or refusal. ***No**, you may not have more dessert.*

# *L*

**LAIN**: past participle of lie; be situated; recline. *The cat had **lain** across the chair to take a nap.*
**LANE**: a narrow way or passage between hedges, fences, walls, or houses. *The right **lane** of a highway is for passing traffic.*

∾

**LAY**: to put or place in a horizontal position or position of rest; set down. ***Lay** the bouquet at the foot of the stairs.*
**LEI**: a wreath of flowers, leaves, etc. for the neck or head. *They received a **lei** upon arriving at the luau.*

∾

**LEAK**: an unintended hole or crack through which liquid, gas, or light escapes. *The garden hose has sprung a **leak**.*
**LEEK**: a plant allied to the onion having a cylindrical bulb and leaves used in cooking. *The recipe included a finely-sliced **leek** for added flavor.*

∾

**LEASED**: to grant a lease, to let rent. *They **leased** the apartment together.*
**LEAST**: the smallest amount or degree. *They bought the **least** amount of lumber available.*

∾

**LESSEN**: to become less, to reduce. *Adding ice to a sprain will **lessen** the pain.*
**LESSON**: a section into which a course of study is divided. *The teacher listed a new **lesson** on the board once a week.*

∾

**LOAN**: money given temporarily. *I am applying for a home equity **loan** through my bank.*
**LONE**: being alone without company. *The robbery was committed by a **lone** gunman.*

∾

**LOOT**: anything taken by dishonesty, force, or stealth. *The **loot** from the burned out building was returned to the owner.*
**LUTE**: a stringed musical instrument having a long and hollow pear-shaped body and vaulted back. *She played the **lute** for the small crowd of music lovers.*

**LINKS**: components or connections as in golf. *She supplied her students with* **links** *to the pertinent information.*

**LYNX**: a type of wildcat having long limbs, a short tail, and tufted ears. *The city zoo has a new* **lynx** *on exhibit for the next month, be sure to visit.*

# *M*

**MADE**: past tense of make (to cause to happen; to bring into being; to form); invented or made up. *We made a large salad with dressing for lunch today.*
**MAID**: a female servant. *The household maid is responsible for cleaning the kitchen after the party.*

༝

**MAIL**: letters or packages sent or delivered by means of the postal system. *Please mail those letters for me today.*
**MALE**: A man; a person bearing an X and Y chromosome pair in the cell nuclei. *The new clerk at the phone store is a male.*

༝

**MAIN**: chief in size or importance. *The presentation will be in the main conference room.*
**MANE**: the long hair growing on the back of or around the neck of an animal, as a horse or lion. *Upon further inspection the horse had a dark brown mane.*
**MEIN**: Chinese wheat flour noodles. *We always order chow mein when we go to our favorite Chinese restaurant.*

༝

**MAIZE**: a pale yellow resembling the color of corn. *The sunflowers were the color of maize.*
**MAZE**: a confusing network of intercommunicating paths or passages. *The old house had a maze running through its back garden.*

༝

**MALL**: a large retail complex containing a variety of stores or shops. *We are going to the mall to shop on Saturday.*
**MAUL**: (n) a heavy hammer. *He used the maul to pound in the stakes.*
(v) to handle roughly. *They were concerned that the large dog would maul the puppy.*

༝

**MARSHALL**: a trusted member of the courts. *The federal marshall was sitting in the courtroom.*
**MARTIAL**: having to do with armed hostilities; warlike. *Martial law was declared on the war-torn city.*

༝

**MAT**: a piece of fabric used as a protective cover. *Please place the dish on the mat.*
**MATTE**: having a dull or lusterless surface. *The table was round with a matte finish.*

**MEAT**: the edible part of flesh of animals, specifically mammals as opposed to fish or poultry, used for food; the edible part of a piece of fruit or a nut. *The* **meat** *spoiled from sitting in the sun.*
**MEET**: to become acquainted with; be introduced to. *Come* **meet** *my friends.*
**METE**: to distribute or apportion by measure. *We will* **mete** *the punishment to fit the crime.*

൙

**MEDAL**: a flat piece of metal bearing an inscription or design or a religious image. *The girl wore a* **medal** *honoring St. Francis.*
**MEDDLE**: to involve oneself in a matter without right or invitation. *You should not* **meddle** *in your friends' affairs.*

൙

**MIGHT**: past tense of may (to be allowed or permitted; to express contingency or desire); ability or power. *We* **might** *have been able to see the movie if we had arrived earlier.*
**MITE**: a small insect. *Be sure to remove the* **mites** *before bringing the plant indoors.*

൙

**MINCE**: to chop up. **Mince** *the garlic before adding it to the sauce.*
**MINTS**: aromatic herbs; flavored candies. **Mints** *are perfect for an after-dinner treat.*

൙

**MINER**: a person who works in a mine. *The* **miner** *was trapped for 12 hours in the mine.*
**MINOR**: lesser, as in size; not serious or important; under the legal age of full responsibility. *The curfew was set in place for a* **minor** *to obey.*

൙

**MISSED**: fail or make a mistake. *She* **missed** *the train and was late arriving at work.*
**MIST**: a cloud of particles made up of globules of water suspended in the atmosphere at or near the Earth's surface. *Spray your houseplants with a fine* **mist** *of water to keep them healthy.*

൙

**MOAN**: a prolonged, low inarticulate sound uttered as if from physical suffering. *The* **moan** *that escaped from her was low and piercing.*
**MOWN**: cut short as in a lawn. *The freshly* **mown** *lawn made me sneeze.*

**MOAT**: a deep wide trench usually filled with water surrounding a fortified place as a castle. *The castle was surrounded by a* **moat** *of chocolate in her dream.*
**MOTE**: a small particle or a speck. *When the sun shines in that window, you can see each and every* **mote** *in the air.*

∽

**MORAL**: concerned with the principles or rules of right conduct. *We all have* **moral** *obligations to which we must adhere.*
**MORALE**: the emotional or mental condition with respect to cheerfulness in the face of opposition. *Positive affirmations keep up our* **morale** *during times of crisis.*

∽

**MORNING**: the first part of the day extending from dawn, or midnight, to noon. *Morning will soon be here.*
**MOURNING**: the manifestation of sorrow for a person's death. *The family is* **mourning** *the death of their patriarch.*

∽

**MUSCLE**: a tissue composed of cells or fibers found in the body. *A* **muscle** *strain should be treated immediately.*
**MUSSEL**: any bivalve mollusk that's edible, such as a barnacle, clam, etc. *We topped off the spaghetti dish we served with a favorite* **mussel** *recipe.*

∽

**MUSTARD**: a pungent powder or paste prepared from the seed of the mustard plant. *Hot dogs taste best when you smother them in* **mustard**.
**MUSTERED**: assembled as for battle; gathered or summoned. *They* **mustered** *the strength to climb the hill after their hike in the woods.*

# *N-O*

**NAVAL**: of or pertaining to warships. *The fleet of **naval** warships was heading toward the gulf.*
**NAVEL**: the umbilicus; the central point or middle of any thing or place. *She **pierced** her navel on a coral reef while swimming.*

ॐ

**NAY**: a denial or refusal. *The tallied vote was registered as 10 ayes and 12 **nays**.*
**NEIGH**: the cry of a horse; a whinny. *Leading the horse off to the side of the lane caused him to **neigh**.*

ॐ

**NONE**: no one; not one. *They looked for more blankets, but **none** were available.*
**NUN**: a woman member of a religious order usually bound by vows of poverty and chastity. *The new **nun** was teaching a first-grade class.*

ॐ

**OAR**: a long shaft with a broad blade at one end used for rowing. *They couldn't go fishing because the **oar** was missing from the rowboat.*
**ORE**: a metal-bearing mineral or rock. *On their recent climbing adventure, they came across an **ore**-filled mine.*

ॐ

**ONE**: being or amounting to a single unit or individual. ***One** person will win the big jackpot.*
**WON**: finished first; was victorious. *She **won** the raffle and took home the prize.*

# P

**PAIL**: a bucket. *They used the **pail** of water for cooking at the campsite.*
**PALE**: lacking intensity of color; colorless or whitish. *After his sickness, his face remained **pale** for a week.*

⚬

**PAIN**: physical suffering or distress due to an injury or illness. *Her **pain** was relieved by taking the aspirin.*
**PANE**: one of the divisions of a window or the like. *Only one **pane** of the window was decorated.*

⚬

**PAIR**: two identical, similar, or matched things. *She bought a new **pair** of shoes for the dance.*
**PARE**: to cut off the outer coating or layer. ***Pare** the apple before slicing it for the pie.*
**PEAR**: an edible fruit. *I'll have a **pear** with my lunch tomorrow.*

⚬

**PALATE**: the roof of the mouth. *She burned her **palate** while drinking a hot liquid.*
**PALETTE**: a thin and usually oval board with a thumbhole at one end used by painters. *The **palette** was filled with brightly-colored paints.*

⚬

**PATIENCE**: the ability or willingness to suppress restlessness or annoyance. *I have very little **patience** when it comes to dealing with children.*
**PATIENTS**: people or animals who are under medical care or treatment. *The doctor's office was filled with **patients**.*

⚬

**PAUSE**: a temporary stop or rest, especially in speech or action. *You should **pause** and look around before crossing a street.*
**PAWS**: the foot of an animal having claws. *The dog's **paws** were dirty from playing in the mud.*

⚬

**PEACE**: the non-warring condition of a nation. *At times of strife, we pray for **peace**.*
**PIECE**: a separate or limited portion. *May I have a **piece** of cake?*

**PEAL**: a loud prolonged ringing of bells. *A **peal** of thunder caused them to react quickly.*

**PEEL**: to strip something of its skin, rind, or bark. *He didn't like to eat the **peel** of the apple.*

❧

**PEARL**: a small rounded bead formed within the shells of certain mollusks; a gem. *The **pearl** was placed in an antique setting for the ring.*

**PURL**: to knit with a reverse stitch. *The entire row was made up of **purl** stitches.*

❧

**PEER**: a person who is equal to another in abilities, qualifications, age, background, and social status. *Some children have a problem dealing with **peer** pressure.*

**PIER**: a structure built on posts extending from land over water and used as a landing place for ships. *He docked the boat at the **pier** while shopping for bait.*

❧

**PIQUED** – a feeling of irritation or resentment. *She **piqued** his interest in the macabre with the scary story.*

**PEAKED** – reached the highest point. *The bridge traffic **peaked** during rush hour.*

**PEEKED** – to sneak a look at or to glimpse. *He saw the dog when he **peeked** through the hole in the fence.*

❧

**PLACE**: a particular portion of space. *There is a **place** downtown where you can buy books.*

**PLAICE**: a European flatfish. *The restaurant is serving **plaice** and rice as their special entree this evening.*

❧

**PLAIN**: clear or distinct to the eye. *The damaged pipe was in **plain** view in the flooded building.*

**PLANE**: a flat or level surface. *The carpenter used his **plane** to level the door.*

❧

**PLUM**: a deep purple fruit. *Eating a **plum** can satisfy an urge to eat something sweet.*

**PLUMB**: true according to a plumb line; perpendicular; absolute. *The builder made sure the windows were **plumb** with the frames.*

**PORE**: to read or study with steady attention; a minute opening as in the skin. *They needed to **pore** over the material for the test on Wednesday.*
**POUR**: to send liquid flowing or falling. ***Pour** the salt slowly into the shaker before setting the table for dinner.*

∽

**PRAISE**: the act of expressing approval or admiration. *They always **praise** people for good deeds.*
**PRAYS**: offers devotion to God or an object of worship. *The family always **prays** before eating a meal.*

∽

**PRIDE**: a high or inordinate opinion of one's own dignity, importance, or merit. *She took **pride** in the work she performed for the nonprofit association.*
**PRIED**: inquired impertinently or unnecessarily into something; looked closely. *He never should have **pried** into their business.*

∽

**PRINCIPAL**: the amount borrowed or still owed on a loan; the owner of a private company. *There is still a large **principal** sum owed on the property.*
**PRINCIPLE**: an accepted or professed rule of action or conduct; a fundamental tenet. *He refused to help the woman on the **principle** of the matter.*

∽

**PROFIT**: a gain or advantage. *There is a huge **profit** to be made from selling those stocks.*
**PROPHET**: a person who speaks for God or a deity, or by divine inspiration. *The young entrepreneur was labeled a modern-day **prophet**.*

# *R*

**RAIN**: water that is condensed from the aqueous vapor in the atmosphere and falls to earth. *The rain fell all day in the flooded area.*
**REIGN**: the period during which a sovereign occupies the throne. *Who will reign as the prom queen?*
**REIN**: leather strap fastened to the end of the bit of a bridle used to control a horse. *Rein the horse in slowly.*

❧

**RAISE**: to move to a higher position; lift up. *Raise the hem of the skirt up slightly.*
**RAYS**: narrow beams of light. *The rays of the sun reflecting from the pool were magnificent.*
**RAZE**: to tear down; demolish. *They will raze the condemned building on Monday.*

❧

**RAPT**: deeply engrossed or absorbed. *The students paid rapt attention to the storyteller.*
**WRAPPED**: to enclose in something wound or folded about. *She wrapped the birthday present in pretty, bright paper.*

❧

**READ**: to look carefully so as to understand the meaning of. *Let's read the new adventure book together.*
**REED**: the straight stalk of any of various tall grasses. *The plank was made from the same material as the reeds growing nearby.*

❧

**REVIEW**: the process of going over an article again in study or recitation to fix facts. *Review the lesson before writing your assignment.*
**REVUE**: a form of theatrical entertainment in which events are parodied. *The play received a smashing revue from the new critic.*

❧

**RHYME**: a word agreeing with another in terminal sound. *Not all poetry is written as a rhyme.*
**RIME**: an opaque coating of tiny, white granular ice particles cause by rapid freezing. *The rime was thick on the outdated meals in the freezer.*

**RING**: a typically circular ban of metal or other durable material for wearing on a finger. *Wearing a **ring** can signify many things.*
**WRING**: to twist forcibly. *Make sure to **wring** all of the water out of the blanket.*

∽

**RITE**: a formal ceremonial act or procedure that's customary in a religious service. *They shared their daughter's **rite** of baptism with the small community.*
**RIGHT**: in accordance with what is good, proper, or just. *We don't always do the **right** thing in emergency situations.*
**WRIGHT**: a person skilled in an art; a craftsperson. *She started her career as a **playwright** when she was a young lady.*
**WRITE**: to trace or form letters or characters on a material with a pen, pencil, or other instrument. *He sat down to **write** a letter to his father.*

∽

**ROAD**: a long narrow stretch with a paved surface. *The **road** surface was covered in dirt.*
**RODE**: past tense of ride (to move along in any way.) *They **rode** in silence to the theater.*
**ROWED**: past tense of row (to move a boat with a paddle). *They **rowed** their way back to the waterfall.*

∽

**ROLE**: part or character played by an actor or actress. *What **role** did he play in acquiring the new client?*
**ROLL**: to move along a surface by revolving or turning over and over as a ball. ***Roll** that log over to the fireplace.*

∽

**ROOT**: a part of the body of a plant that grows downward into the soil. *Make sure the **root** of the plant faces downward.*
**ROUTE**: a course, way, or road for passage or travel. *Which **route** are you taking to the parade?*

∽

**ROSE**: the flower of any such shrub of red, pink, white, or yellow color. *She received one red **rose** after her performance.*
**ROWS**: a number of persons or things arranged in a straight line. *Our group will be sitting in **rows** 10 through 15.*

**ROTE**: routine; a fixed, habitual procedure. *Lunch at noontime is a part of their daily* **rote**.

**WROTE**: past tense of write. *She* **wrote** *a letter of apology for her part in the fight.*

∽

**RYE**: a widely cultivated cereal grass. *We are using* **rye** *flour to make that bread.*

**WRY**: Dryly humorous, often with irony; abnormally bent or turned to one side; twisted. *The comedian was known for his* **wry** *wit.*

# S

**SAIL**: a piece of canvas or other fabric that catches the wind on a boat. *The boat's* **sail** *was torn.*
**SALE**: the act of selling, a special disposal of goods. *The bake* **sale** *was a huge success.*

∽

**SCENE**: the place where some action or event occurs. *That particular* **scene** *took hours to film.*
**SEEN**: past participle of see; perceived with the eyes; looked at. *He was* **seen** *crossing the street at the corner.*

∽

**SEA**: a large body of water. *On the second day of their vacation, they sailed the* **sea** *all day.*
**SEE**: to perceive with the eyes. **See** *if the waitress is ready to take our order.*

∽

**SEAM**: a line where two objects are connected. *The* **seam** *in her new dress ripped open.*
**SEEM**: to appear; to give the impression. *Do they* **seem** *to be having a hard time moving that table?*

∽

**SEAS**: the salt waters that cover the greater part of the earth's surface. *Piracy takes place on the high* **seas** *at times.*
**SEIZE**: to take hold of suddenly or forcibly. *Don't try to* **seize** *the handle while the machine is moving.*

∽

**SERGE**: a twilled worsted or woolen fabric used for clothing. *His suit was made with a blue* **serge** *material.*
**SURGE**: a strong wavelike movement. *She always got a fresh* **surge** *of energy when she exercised.*

∽

**SEW**: to join or attach by stitches. *My grandmother likes to* **sew** *new outfits for me to wear.*
**SO**: in the manner indicated; because of the reason given; to a great extent. *Why are you* **so** *touchy about that subject?*
**SOW**: to scatter seed over the land for growth. *October is a great time to* **sow** *certain crops.*

**SHEAR**: to cut. *They can **shear** a sheep in a couple of minutes.*
**SHEER**: transparently thin as some fabrics. *The curtain material she chose is a **sheer** fabric.*

∽

**SHONE**: past participle of shine (glow with light; shed or cast light). *The light **shone** down from over the tops of their heads.*
**SHOWN**: past participle of show (to exhibit something). *He was **shown** the photos before they were printed.*

∽

**SIDE**: one of the surfaces forming the outside of or bounding a thing. *Only place the logo on one **side** of the product.*
**SIGHED**: to let one's breath out audibly. *He **sighed** loudly and then closed his eyes.*

∽

**SIGHS**: plural of sigh (to let one's breath out audibly). *His **sighs** were quiet and subdued.*
**SIZE**: the dimensions or bulk of anything. *What **size** ring do you wear?*

∽

**SLAY**: to kill by violence. *When they were children, they would play "**Slay** the dragon."*
**SLEIGH**: a light vehicle on runners for transporting over snow and ice. *They went for a **sleigh** ride on Christmas Eve.*

∽

**SLEIGHT**: skill or dexterity; cunning; craft. *The magician used **sleight** of hand during most of his performance.*
**SLIGHT**: a small amount; of little importance. *There was a **slight** difference in the way she spoke after attending a public-speaking seminar.*

∽

**SLOE**: a small, sour blackish fruit. *She put a little bit of **sloe** in the punch to create a different flavor.*
**SLOW**: moving or proceeding with little or less than usual speed. ***Slow** down before you hurt yourself.*

∽

**SOAR**: to fly upward as a bird. *He dreamed that he could **soar** like an eagle.*
**SORE**: physically painful or sensitive as a wound. *His elbow was **sore** from banging it on the doorframe.*

**SOLE**: being the only one. *She is the **sole** heir to her family's fortune.*
**SOUL**: the spiritual part of humans believed to survive death. *He poured his **soul** out to the therapist.*

∽

**SOME**: being an undetermined or unspecified one. *Will you have **some** wine and celebrate with us?*
**SUM**: the aggregate of two or more numbers. *Fifty is the **sum** of 25 times two.*

∽

**SON**: a male child. *Her **son** graduated with honors from high school.*
**SUN**: the star that is the central body of the solar system. *The **sun** was shining brightly today.*

∽

**SPADE**: a tool with an iron blade used for digging. *She uses a **spade** to dig in her garden.*
**SPAYED**: having had the ovaries removed (an animal). *They had their pet **spayed** to keep her from having more pups.*

∽

**STAIR**: one of a flight or series of steps going from one level to another. *Take one **stair** one step at a time when you go to the next floor.*
**STARE**: to gaze fixedly and intently with the eyes wide open. *When you **stare** at someone, you make them uncomfortable.*

∽

**STAKE**: a stick or a post pointed at one end for driving into the ground. *They drove the first **stake** into the ground at daybreak.*
**STEAK**: a slice of meat or fish, especially beef, cooked by broiling, or frying. *She ordered a baked potato to eat with her **steak**.*

∽

**STATIONARY**: standing still; not moving. *He rode a **stationary** bike as part of his exercise regimen.*
**STATIONERY**: writing paper. *The **stationery** she used was monogrammed.*

∽

**STEAL**: to take without permission. *Only a horrible person would **steal** from a church.*
**STEEL**: any of various modified forms of iron artificially produced. *The **steel** mill closed down last year.*

**STEP**: a movement made by lifting the foot and setting down again in a new position. *Take a* **step** *forward and claim your prize.*
**STEPPE**: a large plain; grassland; prairie. *Certain* **steppe** *grasslands can be found in Europe.*

∽

**STILE**: a series of steps or rungs for passing over a wall or a fence that is a barrier for cattle. *The little boy used a* **stile** *for climbing the fence to get in the castle.*
**STYLE**: a fashion or manner. She had lots of style for a plain woman.

∽

**SUITE**: a number of things forming a series or a set. *We stayed in a huge* **suite** *when we visited the Capitol in Washington, D.C.*
**SWEET**: having the taste or flavor of sugar or honey. *The candy was slightly* **sweet** *and satisfied the baby completely.*

# *T*

**TACKS**: short, sharp pointed nails usually with a flat broad head. *I will use some small tacks to keep the carpet from sliding.*
**TAX**: a sum of money demanded by the government for its support. *When will the new tax become a law?*

∽

**TAIL**: the hindmost part of an animal. *The cat caught her tail in the door.*
**TALE**: a narrative that relates the detail of an event or incident. *He told a tale about an experience from his childhood.*

∽

**TARE**: the weight of the wrapping or receptacle containing goods. *Always allow for the tare when you weigh food.*
**TEAR**: to rip or cut. *Tear up the paper that you are not using.*

∽

**TAUGHT**: past tense of teach (to educate). *Her teacher taught Spanish to her brother last year.*
**TAUT**: tightly drawn. *The paper was pulled taut around the packages.*

∽

**TEARS**: a drop of saline, watery fluid secreted from the eye. *She cried tears of joy during the wedding ceremony.*
**TIERS**: one of a series of rows or ranks rising one behind or above another. *The birthday cake consisted of three tiers.*

∽

**THEIR**: a form of the possessive case used as an attributive adjective; belonging to them. *Tell them to keep their gloves in their pockets.*
**THERE**: in or at that place. *Put the mail over there on the table.*
**THEY'RE**: a contraction of "they are". *They're going to the concert together.*

∽

**THREW**: to propel from the hand by a sudden forward motion. *He threw the baseball to the catcher.*
**THROUGH**: in at one end, side or surface and out the other. *Go through that door to reach the classroom.*

**TIC**: a sudden spasmodic involuntary muscular contraction. *When he was stressed, he developed a **tic** on the right side of his face.*
**TICK**: a slight, sharp recurring click, tap, or beat, as of a clock. *She grew more anxious with each **tick** of the clock.*

*પ્ર*

**TIDE**: the rise and fall of the waters of the ocean. *High **tide** is the best time to fish for cod.*
**TIED**: to bind, fasten, or attach with a cord, string, or the like, drawn together and knotted. *His hands were **tied** behind his back.*

*પ્ર*

**THYME**: a plant or herb belonging to the mint family. *When I make roasted chicken, I always sprinkle it with **thyme**.*
**TIME**: a prescribed or allotted period. *What **time** does the school bus get here?*

*પ્ર*

**TO**: used for expressing motion or direction toward a point. *Move over **to** that side of the room.*
**TOO**: in addition; also. *He can go with us to the movies **too**.*
**TWO**: a cardinal number. *That car has **two** flat tires.*

*પ્ર*

**TOLD**: past tense of tell (narrate). *He **told** the story with a flair.*
**TOLLED**: to ring out; peal, as with a bell. *The belled **tolled** three times on the hour.*

# *V*

**VAIN**: excessively proud of or concerned about one's own appearance, quality, etc. *She became quite **vain** after winning the talent contest.*

**VANE**: a blade in the wheel of a windmill. *The new weather **vane** needs to be attached to the roof as soon as possible.*

**VEIN**: a vessel or tube conveying blood from various parts of the body to the heart. *She accidentally sliced through a **vein** in her hand while cutting the meat.*

⤳

**VALE**: a valley. *The **vale** was beautiful at sunset.*

**VEIL**: a piece of opaque material worn over the face for concealment. *She wore a **veil** that covered the lower portion of her face.*

# *W-Y*

**WAIST**: part of the human body between the ribs and the hips. *The apron was tied around her* **waist**.
**WASTE**: use to no avail or profit; squander. *The* **waste** *in the dumpster was accumulating quickly.*

∽

**WAIT**: to remain inactive or in a state of repose waiting until something unexpected happens. *Just* **wait** *until you see the finished work of art.*
**WEIGHT**: the amount or quantity of heaviness or mass. *His excess* **weight** *was causing a problem with his health.*

∽

**WAIVE**: to refrain from claiming or insisting on; give up. *Can I* **waive** *the insurance coverage that I don't need?*
**WAVE**: to move back and forth, gesture; sea surf, current. *Be sure to* **wave** *to the children when you pass the school bus.*

∽

**WAR**: a conflict carried on by force of arms; armed conflict. *Our neighborhood has waged a* **war** *on illegal drug use.*
**WORE**: past tense of wear (to be clothed in). *She* **wore** *pink ribbons in her hair.*

∽

**WAY**: a manner, mode, or fashion. *What is the correct* **way** *to hem a skirt?*
**WEIGH**: to measure heaviness. *Be sure to* **weigh** *the meat before wrapping it.*

∽

**WE**: the nominative plural of I. *We will meet at the corner and walk together to the bus stop.*
**WEE**: little; very small. *He was a* **wee** *child when his father died.*

∽

**WEAK**: not strong; liable to break or collapse under pressure or strain. *After the surgery, you will be extremely* **weak**.
**WEEK**: a period of seven successive days. *It will take a* **week** *before the store can ship your order.*

**WEAR**: to carry or have on the body as a covering. *What will you **wear** to the dance?*
**WHERE**: in or at what place. ***Where** do you live?*

∽

**WEATHER**: the state of the atmosphere with respect to wind, temperature, mois-ture, etc. *Let's hope for nice **weather** when the circus comes to town.*
**WETHER**: a castrated male sheep. *The farmer sheared the **wether** a second time to get all of the wool.*
**WHETHER**: used to introduce the first of two or more alternatives (whether to go or not). *Who will decide **whether** or not we will attend the wedding next week?*

∽

**WE'D**: a contraction for "we had", "we should", or "we would". ***We'd** like to invite you to visit us the next time you come to town.*
**WEED**: a valueless plant growing wild. *I never knew that a dandelion was consid-ered a **weed**, did you?*

∽

**WEIR**: a small dam in a river or stream. *The **weir** was damaged by the recent storm.*
**WE'RE**: contraction of "we are". ***We're** ready to proceed to the next step with our cooking lessons.*

∽

**WET**: moistened, covered, or soaked with water or another liquid. *The blanket was **wet** from the recent rain shower.*
**WHET**: to sharpen a knife or tool, etc. by grinding or friction. *He **whet** all of his old tools when he finished cleaning the garage.*

∽

**WHICH**: what one, whichever. ***Which** of those flowers will you choose?*
**WITCH**: a person, especially a woman, who professes to practice magic. *She played a **witch** in the school play.*

∽

**WHINE**: to utter a low, usually nasal, complaining cry or sound. *Don't **whine** when things are not going your way.*
**WINE**: the fermented juice of grapes, usually having an alcoholic content of 14% or less. *Have a glass of **wine** to celebrate your anniversary.*

∽

**WHO'S**: contraction of "who is", "who has". ***Who's** the author of that book?*
**WHOSE**: the possessive case of who used as an adjective. ***Whose** shoes is he wearing?*

**WOOD**: the trunks or main stems of trees. *He used* **wood** *from the broken chair as kindling for the fire.*

**WOULD**: used in place of will to make a statement or form a question less direct or blunt. *Who* **would** *be the better candidate for the position?*

൙

**YOKE**: a device for joining together a pair of draft animals like oxen. *The pair horses were joined together with a wide* **yoke**.

**YOLK**: the yellow and principal substance of an egg. *That recipe includes the* **yolk** *of one egg.*

# *A*bout the Author

Kathy Zengolewicz is a freelance writer and Virtual Assistant (VA). She has been writing non-fiction for 17 years and opened her VA business, The Virtual Independent Contractor, (www.kathyzengolewicz.com), in 2002.

Kathy is a wife, mother and grandmother. She works out of her home office in Philadelphia, PA, where she lives with her husband of 40 years.

Kathy wrote this e-book for anyone who writes, as well as others who are interested in the proper usage of the American English written word.

Enjoy!

www.ingramcontent.com/pod-product-compliance
Lightning Source LLC
Chambersburg PA
CBHW070109070426
42448CB00038B/2460